**Eco-responsible web design.**
**A practical guide to sustainable websites.**

AF143301

# ECO-RESPONSIBLE
# WEB DESIGN
## A practical guide to sustainable websites

Grégory Clément

© 2024 Grégory Clément

Edition: BoD - Books on Demand, info@bod.fr
Printing: BoD – Books on Demand, In de Tarpen 42,
Norderstedt (Germany)

Printing on demand

ISBN : 978-2-3225-3709-9
Legal deposit : April 2024

**Translated from the original French by Deepl.**

# CONTEXT

In the vast world of the web, the notion of sustainable development is becoming increasingly important. Beyond simply reducing environmental impact, it also encompasses social and economic aspects, seeking to strike a balance between present needs and long-term imperatives.

In this context, sustainable web development aims to create and manage websites that meet user expectations while minimizing their ecological footprint. With the rapid growth of digital technology, energy consumption, greenhouse gas emissions and the production of electronic waste have increased significantly. Websites, as essential components of this digital revolution, make a major contribution to these issues. It is therefore crucial to understand and integrate sustainable development practices to mitigate these negative impacts and encourage a transition towards a more responsible web industry.

The main objective of this document is to provide a deeper understanding of the various aspects of sustainable development as applied to the web. By proposing concrete strategies for designing, developing, and maintaining websites while reducing their impact on the environment, this document aims to guide web professionals, developers, project managers and anyone interested towards more sustainable practices.

Ultimately, this book aspires to become a tool for those seeking to harmonize the imperatives of web development with the demands of preserving our planet. By understanding the issues, adopting responsible practices, and fostering a committed community, we can contribute to the advent of a more sustainable Internet that respects our environment.

Every action counts.

# ABOUT THE AUTHOR

Born in 1971, Grégory Clément has been an entrepreneur, author, and speaker in the world of digital communications for over twenty years. After working for major accounts in the automotive, *retail* and e-commerce sectors, the sustainable and eco-responsible aspects of his job have become increasingly important to him. He now wants to pass on the knowledge and experience he has acquired over the years.

Chapter I

# THE FOUNDATIONS OF SUSTAINABLE DEVELOPMENT

Sustainable development is a holistic approach that aims to balance the environmental, social, and economic dimensions of an activity. In the context of the web, these fundamental principles take on particular importance. This chapter explores the fundamentals of sustainable development, focusing on their application to web development and examining the environmental impact of the digital sector.

## UNDERSTAND THE FUNDAMENTAL OF SUSTAINABLE DEVELOPMENT

Sustainable development is based on three essential pillars: economic, social, and environmental. On the economic front, it is about guaranteeing the financial viability of projects.

Socially, it aims to promote equity, diversity, and the well-being of individuals. Finally, on the environmental side, the aim is to minimize negative impacts on the planet. Applying these principles to web development means designing sites that thrive economically, respect users' rights and minimize their ecological footprint.

# ENVIRONMENTAL IMPACT OF THE DIGITAL

The digital revolution has considerably increased energy demand, mainly due to the data centers that power websites. Greenhouse gas emissions, water consumption and the production of electronic waste are also major concerns.

The environmental impact of the digital sector is significant and continues to grow as reliance on technology increases. Here are some key figures to illustrate the scale of this impact:

**Energy consumption:**
- According to *the International Energy Agency* (IEA)[1] , global electricity consumption due to information and communication technologies (ICTs) represents around 1 to 2% of total electricity consumption.
- Data centers, which host a large proportion of online services, are responsible for a significant proportion of this consumption. In 2020, they accounted for around 200 terawatt hours (TWh) of electricity per year, or almost 1% of global electricity consumption.

---

[1]  International Energy Agency: https://www.iea.org

**Greenhouse gas emissions:**
- The digital sector generates a significant amount of green-house gas emissions. According to the *Global e-Sustainability Initiative* (GeSI)[2] , direct emissions from the digital sector represented around 1.4% of global GHG emissions in 2020.

- Indirect emissions, mainly linked to the manufacture and disposal of electronic equipment and the production of electricity, are also significant.

**Production of electronic waste:**
- The rapid growth of technology is leading to an increase in electronic waste. In 2019, the world generated around 53.6 million tons of e-waste, and this figure is expected to rise as more and more electronic devices are produced and disposed of, according to the *Global E-Waste Monitor Report*[3] .

**Water consumption:**
- The production and cooling of electronic equipment, as well as the extraction of the materials needed to manu-facture it, contribute to water consumption[4] . Although this amount is relatively small compared to other sectors, it is not negligible and could become more of a concern as demand for technology increases.

---

[2] Global e-Sustainability Initiative (GeSI): https://gesi.org
[3] Global E-Waste Monitor Report: https://www.globalewaste.org
[4] United Nations Information and Communication Technologies for Environment and Health (UNU-INWEH): https://inweh.unu.edu

Understanding these impacts is crucial to developing appropriate and sustainable solutions. Choices in web development can help to mitigate these problems, while guaranteeing optimum performance. The challenge now is to lay the foundations for a transition to a digital industry that is more respectful of the environment and socially responsible.

Sustainable web development starts with ethical and responsible design. This includes reducing energy consumption and integrating fair practices throughout the development process. Technological choices, programming languages and site architectures need to be assessed for their impact on sustainability.

# THE TRAP OF "NO-CODE NO-CODE" PLATFORMS

When it comes to creating a content site - by which we mean excluding e-commerce platforms and other interfaces with third-party software such as CRM or ERP, where a certain level of technical expertise is required - there are now many possibilities thanks to online solutions such as *Wix*, *SquareSpace*, *Webly*, *Podia*, *Jimdo* and many others, the list is long.

These '*no-code*' platforms offer real added value in terms of functionality and design, and above all they require no technical knowledge of web development. All you must do is let yourself be guided by their increasingly intuitive interfaces to build your content pages one by one. It's a tempting solution.

However, these platforms do little or nothing to address the three pillars of sustainable development:

- **Economic pillar.** These are private pay platforms. To use them, you must pay a monthly fee, sometimes a large sum, with no guarantee of full ownership of the data or of the continuity of the service. Open source is preferable.

- **Social pillar.** Some of these platforms offer the basics of accessibility, but they fall far short of the mark, particularly when it comes to the transparency of customer data. As for the GDPR rules (respect for visitor privacy), they do not apply to platforms outside the European Union.

- **Environmental pillar.** This pillar is currently partially or completely ignored. There is little data on the quality of hosting servers and their sustainable management, on constant improvements in the use of bandwidth and the management of content quality, or on the optimization of the source code of the pages consulted.

It's true that we won't achieve a zero-carbon footprint for the time being, but there are already plenty of opportunities for improvement, all of which are inexpensive and perfectly accessible to novices.

Chapter II

# ECO-DESIGN
# OF WEBSITES

The eco-design of websites is an essential approach to integrating the principles of sustainable development right from the design and development phase and is based on taking environmental issues into account throughout a site's life cycle. This includes the design, development, hosting, and even end-of-life phases. The aim is to minimize the consumption of resources, optimize performance and reduce the overall impact on the environment.

To integrate eco-design into the development process, several basic practices are essential. These include optimizing source code to reduce consumption of server resources, reducing page weight to reduce bandwidth consumption, and using energy-efficient technologies.

# HTML/CSS/JAVASCRIPT

Basically, it is quite possible to create a simple website using HTML, CSS and JavaScript rendering languages. This is what Content Management System platforms deliver to visitors, since these are the only languages recognized and interpreted by web browsers. But although these languages are accessible to everyone and can be used quickly, thanks to the many libraries of examples available online, developing a complete content site using this technology quickly becomes time-consuming.

The first obstacle is the navigation zones and footers that appear on each page. A simple textual modification requires the code of all these pages to be reviewed. The need to use server code to encapsulate these recurring code elements in snippets is quickly felt.

Another problem quickly arises when you need to manage a contact form or newsletter subscription. Server code quickly becomes unavoidable for even the most basic functions.

To do this, it is possible to add a PHP-type code engine for the most extensive and probably the most affordable technically, or even a MySQL-type database if the need arises to record data used or collected.

That's why content management platforms (CMS) have been around since the early 2000s. With a single installation and a few clicks, everything was in place and ready to use. Some platforms were paid for, others were free (open source).

# THE CHOICE OF OPEN SOURCE

Open source refers to an approach to software development where the source code is made available to the public. This means that anyone can examine, modify, and distribute the software's source code. Open-source projects are often developed collaboratively, with contributions from developers around the world. This approach promotes transparency, customization, flexibility and security.

Open-source software can be seen as a sustainable solution in several respects.

1. **Community collaboration.** Open-source projects often involve the collaboration of a worldwide community of developers. This collaborative approach enables continuous improvement, bug fixes and updates, leading to software that can adapt to changing needs and technologies.

2. **Longevity.** The open-source model tends to favor the long-term sustainability of software. If the original people responsible for a project move on, other members of the community can take over to continue development and support.

3. **Customization and flexibility.** Open-source software allows users to modify the source code to meet specific requirements. This flexibility allows organizations to adapt

the software to their needs without relying on a single supplier.

4. **Cost effectiveness.** Open source often reduces costs for businesses and individuals. It eliminates license fees and allows users to avoid being locked in by a supplier, promoting a more profitable and sustainable model.

5. **Security.** The transparency of open-source code enables constant monitoring, making it easier to identify and correct security vulnerabilities. This collaborative approach to security helps to create more robust software. If a vulnerability is discovered, it is quickly corrected and deployed.

6. **Reduced resource consumption.** Open-source software tends to be resource-efficient, allowing it to run on a variety of hardware configurations. This can result in lower hardware requirements and reduced energy consumption compared to resource-hungry proprietary alternatives.

However, it is important to note that sustainability is a complex and multifaceted concept. While open source can contribute positively to sustainability, other factors such as hardware choice, energy efficiency and development practices also play crucial roles. In addition, the sustainability of an open-source project can depend on ongoing community involvement, financial support and commitment to maintaining and improving the software over time. A case in point is

*Joomla*, an open-source CMS (for *Content Management System*) that looked promising a few years ago but has been abandoned over the years in favor of simpler-to-maintain platforms such as Wordpress or Drupal. The result is a somewhat restricted community of developers and, consequently, higher development, deployment, and maintenance costs than current market standards.

# WORDPRESS, THE ULTIMATE CMS?

WordPress is now considered to be an essential CMS for creating content websites. There are several reasons for this, which have contributed to its success and widespread adoption as a content management platform.

WordPress was born in 2003 when Mike Little and Matt Mullenweg created a derivative version of *b2evolution*[5] . The need for an elegant, well-designed personal publishing system was obvious even then. Today, WordPress is built on PHP and MySQL and is licensed under GPLv2. It is also the platform chosen by over 43% of all websites[6].

WordPress has evolved progressively over time, supported by skilled and enthusiastic developers, designers, scientists, bloggers, and many others. People with limited technical experience can use it "out of the box", and the more experienced can customize it in remarkable ways, thanks to:

- **Ease of use**
  WordPress is renowned for its user-friendliness and ease of use. Even users without advanced technical skills can create and manage websites efficiently thanks to its intuitive interface.

_____

[5] https://b2evolution.net
[6] https://wordpress.org

- **Large community**
  WordPress has a vast community of users, developers, and contributors. This dynamic community provides technical support, themes, plugins, and resources that contribute to the continuous improvement of the platform.

- **Flexibility and scalability**
  WordPress offers great flexibility thanks to its themes and plugins. You can customize the look and functionality of a site by using pre-built themes or by creating custom designs. Plugins can be used to add specific functionality as required.

- **Free and open source**
  WordPress is open-source software, which means that it is free to use, and its source code is accessible to everyone. This encourages transparency, customization, and collaboration.

- **SEO** (Search Engine Optimization)
  WordPress is well optimized for search engines, which makes it easier for websites to be found naturally. It also offers dedicated plugins to further improve SEO.

- **Extensive ecosystem of themes and plugins**
  There are a multitude of themes and plugins available for WordPress, allowing users to customize their sites to their specific needs without having to develop everything from scratch.

- **Regular updates and security**

  The active community of developers ensures the security of WordPress by regularly publishing updates. These updates include security patches and enhancements, ensuring a constantly evolving and secure environment, although there are several plugins that significantly increase support for security aspects.

- **Adaptability to different types of sites**

  Whether you need a blog, a business site, an online shop or a portfolio, WordPress can be adapted to different types of site thanks to its versatile features.

Because of these advantages, WordPress has become a popular choice for many users, whether they are individual bloggers, small businesses, or large corporations, reinforcing its position as the must-have platform today.

**Can Wordpress be included in the sustainable development box?**

No, Wordpress itself is not used for its sustainable approach. That is not its vocation. Like all CMS, it runs on the server and is used to create content websites.

It is when the website is rendered on the browsers that its environmental impact can be measured, with the main relays being:

- Choice of hosting server,
- Selection of the theme and plugins used,
- Optimizing rendering performance,
- Sustainability of content,
- Accessibility.

Measuring the environmental impact of a website is therefore crucial for identifying areas where improvements are needed. There are free online tools for this, such as:

- **PageSpeed Insights**[7]
  Based on Google's *Lighthouse* engine[8] , *PageSpeed Insights* (PSI) provides reports on the user experience of a page on mobile devices and computers and suggests improvements to be made to the page.

---

[7] https://pagespeed.web.dev/?hl=fr
[8] https://github.com/GoogleChrome/lighthouse/releases/tag/v11.0.0

PSI provides test data and actual data about a page. Test data is useful for debugging problems, as it is collected in a controlled environment. Although the elements of the reports are somewhat difficult to understand, PSI remains a reliable source for improving page load speed and user experience.

- **Website Carbon**[9]
  This site allows you to calculate the carbon emissions of a website simply by providing its URL.
  The calculation method is described on this page:
  https://sustainablewebdesign.org/calculating-digital-emissions/

- **Digital Beacon**[10]
  Digital Beacon is a great tool for analyzing websites. It shows $CO_2$ emissions, page size and lots of useful tips.

- **Ecograder**[11]
  Ecograder is another tool that lets you analyze websites. It also gives you detailed advice on how to make the site more environmentally friendly.

- **The Green Web Foundation**[12]
  Quite comprehensive, this toolkit is first and foremost a foundation working to make the Internet fossil fuel free

_____

[9] https://www.websitecarbon.com
[10] https://digitalbeacon.co
[11] https://ecograder.com
[12] https://www.thegreenwebfoundation.org

by 2030. There is also a system of recognized certifications.

This type of tool is increasingly available on the Internet, and a simple Internet search will reveal many more. These are just a few of the best-known and most useful examples.

# THE CASE OF HEADLESS CMS

In recent years, new content management tools called *Headless CMS have* appeared on the market.

A *Headless CMS* is totally independent of the front-end architecture content management that is generally required when creating websites as a CMS. In simple terms, a *Headless CMS* functions as a digital content repository that enables multi-platform content delivery. It offers content as a service (CaaS), so that content can be created and edited within the CMS infrastructure. At the same time, it makes the raw content available to other systems.

Some of the best *Headless* content management systems are:

- Sanity.io[13] ,
- Contentstack[14] ,
- Contentful[15] ,
- GraphCMS[16] .

In terms of sustainable development, *headless CMSs* could prove to be an interesting alternative because of the complete separation between the back and front offices. Even more since front-end rendering is done using modern

---

[13] https://www.sanity.io

[14] https://www.contentstack.com

[15] https://www.contentful.com

[16] https://graphcms.com

JavaScript frameworks such as *React*, *Vues.js* or *Angular,* to name but a few.

But their full deployment requires solid technical knowledge. What you gain in flexibility and agility, you lose in complexity, cost, and dependency on developers.

Chapter III

# RESPONSIBLE HOSTING

In recent years, the environmental impact of technology has come under intense scrutiny, prompting companies and individuals to look for environmentally friendly alternatives. Sustainable web hosting has emerged as a crucial aspect of reducing the digital carbon footprint. This essay explores the concept of sustainable web hosting, its importance, and provides a list of ten worthy European providers committed to environmentally friendly practices.

Sustainable web hosting involves using environmentally responsible practices to minimize the ecological impact of hosting websites and online services. Traditional data centers, which power the Internet, consume considerable amounts of energy, and contribute significantly to carbon emissions. Sustainable web hosting aims to mitigate these effects through a variety of strategies.

**Here are some aspects to consider when making an eco-responsible choice:**

1. **Use of Renewable Energy**
   Sustainable web hosting providers favor the use of renewable energy sources such as solar, wind or hydro power to power their data centers. This transition reduces dependence on fossil fuels, contributing to a greener energy mix.

2. **Energy Efficiency**
   The optimum use of energy-efficient hardware and technology helps to minimize overall energy consumption. This includes the use of energy-efficient servers, efficient cooling systems and energy-efficient lighting in data centers.

3. **Resource Conservation**
   Sustainable web hosting providers seek to minimize wasted resources by implementing practices such as server virtualization, which allows multiple virtual servers to run on a single physical machine, reducing hardware requirements.

4. **Environmental Certifications**
   Many sustainable hosting providers seek certification from recognized and independent environmental organizations, such as the *Green Web Foundation*[17] or the

---

[17] https://www.thegreenwebfoundation.org

*Carbon Trust[18]* . These certifications validate their commitment to environmentally friendly practices.

5. **Carbon offsetting**

   Some web hosts invest in carbon offset projects to neutralize their carbon footprint. This involves supporting initiatives such as reforestation or renewable energy projects to balance the emissions generated by their operations. This aspect, while interesting and commendable, should be considered as a last resort, as it is primarily a matter of compensation and not of real sustainability.

However, the environmental aspect is not the only one to be considered for complete sustainable development.

**Corporate Social Responsibility (CSR).**
Companies are increasingly incorporating sustainability into their CSR initiatives. Opting for sustainable web hosting aligns with these values, demonstrating a commitment to environmental responsibility.

**Consumer Confidence and Preference.**
Consumers are increasingly aware of the environment and are likely to choose companies that share their values. Sustainable web hosting can increase consumer confidence and preference for a website or online service.

**Regulatory Compliance**

---

[18] https://www.carbontrust.com/en-eu

With the proliferation of environmental regulations, companies adopting sustainable practices, including web hosting, can ensure their compliance with ever-changing environmental standards.

Finally, sustainable hosting is not synonymous with compromise or degradation of basic services. The quality of 1st and 2nd level support must be guaranteed.

**Some European sustainable web hosting providers** listed alphabetically.

1. **Kualo**[19] (United Kingdom)
   *Kualo* is renowned for its commitment to 100% renewable energy, offering accommodation services powered by wind and solar energy.

2. **GreenGeeks**[20] (Germany)
   *GreenGeeks* is a recognized leader in green hosting, using energy-efficient equipment and purchasing wind energy credits.

3. **HostEurope**[21] (Germany)
   *HostEurope focuses on* energy-saving practices and is certified by the German Federal Environment Agency for its commitment to sustainability.

---

[19] https://www.kualo.com
[20] https://www.greengeeks.com
[21] https://www.hosteurope.de/en

4. **EasyHost**[22] (Belgium)
   *EasyHost* focuses on energy-efficient servers and uses green energy, helping to reduce environmental impact.

5. **Eco Hosting**[23] (United Kingdom)
   As its name suggests, *Eco Hosting* provides environmentally friendly hosting solutions based on renewable energy sources.

6. **Infomaniak**[24] (Switzerland)
   *Infomaniak* is 100% powered by renewable energy and actively participates in reforestation projects to offset its carbon footprint.

7. **Green.ch**[25] (Switzerland)
   *Green.ch* focuses on sustainable practices and has been awarded certifications for its commitment to energy-efficient and environmentally friendly accommodation.

8. **Datacampus**[26] (France)
   Located in Poitiers, *Datacampus* uses a cooling system based on recycled water. Its energy consumption is modelled on that of Futuroscope, which it shares premises with.

---

[22] https://www.easyhost.be/en
[23] https://www.ecohosting.co.uk
[24] https://www.infomaniak.com/fr
[25] https://www.green.ch/en
[26] https://datacampus.fr

9. **One.com**[27] (Denmark)

One.com is an 'old' web host, probably one of the cheapest. They have recently started offering a green alternative that needs to be tested.

**Good to know**: The *Green Web Foundation* provides a directory of green hosting companies. The *Green Web Directory*[28] is a searchable list that allows users to quickly find verified green hosting companies. These are organizations that offer hosting services and can demonstrate that they are taking steps to avoid, reduce or offset greenhouse gas emissions caused using electricity to provide their services. However, this free service is still in beta version.

**Compliance with the General Data Protection Regulation.**

There is no incompatibility between hosting in Switzerland or the UK and the rules of the General Data Protection Regulation (GDPR). Both countries are not members of the European Union (EU), but they provide equivalent data protection through their own legislation, in particular the *Federal Data Protection Act*[29] (DPA) for Switzerland and *The Data Protection Act 2018*[30] , its equivalent in the UK.

If the hosting provider complies with data protection standards, it can be considered as offering an adequate level of

---

[27] https://www.one.com/en/hosting/green-hosting

[28] https://app.greenweb.org/directory/

[29] https://www.kmu.admin.ch/kmu/fr/home/faits-et-tendances/digitalisation/protection-des-donnees/nouvelle-loi-sur-la-protection-des-donnees-nlpd.html

[30] https://www.gov.uk/data-protection

protection, like the GDPR standards. However, it is important to ensure that it has appropriate measures in place to guarantee the security of personal information, and that it can provide the necessary guarantees in accordance with the GDPR.

Chapter IV

# PERFORMANCE OPTIMISATION

When it comes to providing an optimal user experience on a website, speed and responsiveness are essential. Optimizing website performance starts with optimizing page load speed and reducing bandwidth consumption. Page load speed has a significant impact on the user experience, but it also plays a crucial role in a website's energy consumption and carbon footprint. Fast pages not only satisfy users - especially from a smartphone - but also reduce the energy demand on servers and network infrastructures. What's more, fast-loading web pages also contribute to better search engine ranking.

# SETTING UP A CACHING SYSTEM

A common method of optimizing the loading time of a website is to set up a cache system. A cache is a mechanism that temporarily stores frequently used data to reduce the time taken to access that data. On a website, this means saving certain pages or page elements so that they do not have to be recalculated or retrieved each time a new request is made. In other words, the cache makes it possible to serve pre-generated static content instead of dynamically rebuilding the page on each visit.

There are several types of cache:

1. The **browser cache.**
   The browser-side cache stores resources locally on the user's computer - or smartphone. This includes CSS files, JavaScript, images, etc. When a user returns to a page, the browser can load these resources from the local cache rather than downloading them again from the server. Make sure that static resources such as CSS, JavaScript and images are configured to be cached on the browser side. This is done by defining appropriate headers in server responses, telling the browser how long it can keep these files in cache. The principle of private browsing, available on all modern browsers, allows you to bypass this caching system and view the latest modifications. Useful for all webmasters and content editors.

2. The **server cache.**

   The server-side cache stores copies of complete pages or page fragments on the server. This reduces the load on the server by avoiding the need to recalculate pages for each request. Tools such as *Varnish*[31] or *Nginx*[32] can be used to set up a server-side cache. But rest assured, most web hosts have this service natively available. It is then possible to purge it from the hosting user interface.

3. The **database cache.**

   For websites that frequently retrieve data from a database, database-level caching can be used. This can be achieved by storing the results of frequently used queries in memory, reducing the need for repetitive queries. In the case of a Wordpress engine - or other modern CMS - this type of caching is already perfectly in place.

---

[31] https://varnish-cache.org/intro/index.html#intro
[32] https://docs.nginx.com/nginx/admin-guide/content-cache/content-caching/

4. **Dynamic content cache**

   In the case of dynamically generated content in Wordpress - or any other modern CMS - there are sophisticated and effective solutions available via dedicated extensions such as the *WP-rocket*[33] , *WP Super Cache*[34] or *W3 Total Cache*[35] plugins, which can be used to store page fragments or the results of frequent calculations in memory. These solutions are very easy to configure and have a large community of users. What's more, they can be used in parallel with and in addition to a CDN (see below) and use events to trigger the invalidation and purging of the cache, such as the publication of a new article.

5. **Content Delivery Networks (CDNs)**

   CDNs, which optimize the distribution of web content, play a crucial role in the user experience, and their energy impact can be significant.

When a user requests the static resources of a website for the first time, a CDN server transfers the files from the origin server. It also caches a copy of the resources in the server closest to the user, called an edge server, and reuses the stored data for future requests. Caching allows site content to be served to visitors much more quickly and reduces the workload on the web server. If your visitor is from India and your origin server is in Europe, content delivery may take longer because of the physical distance between them.

---

[33] https://wp-rocket.me/

[34] https://wordpress.org/plugins/wp-super-cache/

[35] https://wordpress.org/plugins/w3-total-cache/

Setting up a CDN is very simple. Use a tool such as *CDN Finder*[36] to check whether a CDN is already integrated into your site. Choose between a free or paid CDN service depending on your needs. Most of the time for a classic content website, a free version will be sufficient with, for example, *Cloudflare*[37] . Activate it and test the changes.

With a properly configured CDN alone, site security is enhanced because static data is no longer loaded from the root server, bandwidth usage is reduced because static data is delivered from nearby caches, and search engine ranking is improved thanks to the increase in loading speed.

Here again, the CDN needs to be purged each time the content or code is modified to ensure that the content is always up to date.

Once the cache system is in place, it is crucial to monitor its performance and adjust it if necessary. Monitoring tools such as *Google Analytics / PageSpeed Insights* or tools specific to the hosting server can provide information on cache usage and server response times.

---

[36] https://www.cdnplanet.com/tools/cdnfinder/
[37] https://www.cloudflare.com/fr-fr/

# CORE WEB VITALS: THE GOOGLE METHOD FOR OPTIMISING WEB PERFORMANCE

*Core Web Vitals is a* Google initiative that dates to 2020 and aims to improve the loading speed and user experience (UX) of all websites. With tools such as *PageSpeed Insights*, *Mobile-Friendly Test*, *Lighthouse* among others and broader movements such as AMP, the Chrome UX Report and web.dev, Core Web Vitals seeks to establish simple, unified criteria for what a good web experience is.

*Core Web Vitals is* based on three measures. Each of them addresses an essential aspect of a page's speed and user experience.

- **Largest Contentful Paint** - LCP
  The LCP indicator measures content loading time, marking the exact moment when the largest piece of content - image, video, block of text - above the waterline (what you see without scrolling down) is fully loaded. A good LCP lasts no more than 2.5 seconds.

- **First Input Delay** - FID
  Based on the RAIL (Response Animation Idle Load) framework, the First Input Delay metric measures the responsiveness of the web page. Explicitly, it is the time that elapses between the moment when the user performs an action such as clicking and the moment when the browser responds to this interaction. A good FID should respond in less than 100 milliseconds. NB: this metric is

replaced in March 2024 by INP (Interaction to Next Paint).

- **Cumulative Layout Shift** - CLS
  Cumulative Layout Shift measures visual stability. Often, elements on a page shift as content loads and is displayed on the screen - a rather wearying experience that generally leads to many clicks in the wrong place. This metric quantifies the frequency and extent to which these changes occur on a page.

**To obtain a score close to 100% on *PageSpeed Insights*, here are a few tips:**

1. **Image compression**
   Use pre-compressed images and choose the right format (WebP is often recommended). Use free online tools such as *TinyPNG*[38] to drastically reduce the weight of images without any noticeable loss. Adding a dedicated Worpress plugin is a plus (*Imagify*[39] , *ShortPixel*[40] , *TinyPNG*[38], *EWWW*[41]).

2. **Browser caching**
   Configure an appropriate caching policy to take advantage of browser-side storage. To do this, simply add the following code to your .htaccess file:

---

[38] https://tinypng.com
[39] https://imagify.io/fr/
[40] https://shortpixel.com
[41] https://ewww.io

```
# Expires headers
<IfModule mod_expires.c>
ExpiresActive on
ExpiresDefault "access plus 1 month
# cache.appcache needs re-requests in FF 3.6 (thanks
Remy ~Introducing HTML5)
ExpiresByType text/cache-manifest "access plus 0
seconds
# Your document html
ExpiresByType text/html "access plus 0 seconds
# Data
ExpiresByType text/xml "access plus 0 seconds
ExpiresByType application/xml "access plus 0 seconds
ExpiresByType application/json "access plus 0 seconds
# Feed
ExpiresByType application/rss+xml "access plus 1 hour
ExpiresByType application/atom+xml "access plus 1 hour
# Favicon (cannot be renamed)
ExpiresByType image/x-icon "access plus 1 week
# Media: images, video, audio
ExpiresByType image/gif "access plus 4 months"
ExpiresByType image/png "access plus 4 months"
ExpiresByType image/jpeg "access plus 4 months
ExpiresByType image/webp "access plus 4 months
ExpiresByType video/ogg "access plus 4 months
ExpiresByType audio/ogg "access plus 4 months
ExpiresByType video/mp4 "access plus 4 months
ExpiresByType video/webm "access plus 4 months
# HTC files (css3pie)
ExpiresByType text/x-component "access plus 1 month
# Webfonts
ExpiresByType font/ttf "access plus 4 months
ExpiresByType font/otf "access plus 4 months
ExpiresByType font/woff "access plus 4 months"
ExpiresByType font/woff2 "access plus 4 months"
ExpiresByType image/svg+xml "access plus 1 month
ExpiresByType application/vnd.ms-fontobject "access
plus 1 month"
# CSS and JavaScript
ExpiresByType text/css "access plus 1 year
ExpiresByType application/javascript "access plus 1
year"
</IfModule>
```

If you are using Wordpress and modifying the .htaccess file seems too technical, opt for a dedicated plugin such as *Leverage Browser Caching*[42] .

3. **Minification of CSS, JS, and HTML files**
   Reduce file size by eliminating spaces and comments and minimizing code. Here again, many online tools allow you to do this. But most Wordpress caching plugins incorporate it natively.

4. **Reduction of** HTTP **requests**
   Reduce the number of requests by combining CSS and JS files where possible. Here again, if you're using a Wordpress *Page Builder such as Elementor* or *Divi* (to name only the best performers), this point is probably already in place.

5. **Asynchronous or deferred loading of** resources
   Make sure that the scripts do not block the initial rendering.

6. Font **optimization**
   Use optimized web fonts and limit the number of variants (italic, bold, semi-bold, normal, semi-light or light). To do this, the best option is to choose from the multitude of fonts offered by *Google Font*[43] , which are free of rights and optimized for the web, download them and incorporate them into your site using the script provided.

---

[42] https://wordpress.org/plugins/leverage-browser-caching/
[43] https://fonts.google.com/

Using them directly from the Google Font site penalizes the results in terms of loading speed and optimizing the number of requests. In addition, a usage cookie has been added which you will need to manage in your global cookie list (see accessibility section).

7. **Optimizing the initial rendering**
Priorities the loading of resources required for the initial rendering, for example:

**Critical CSS**: Identify the CSS that is essential to the initial display of the page (above the waterline) and place it directly in the HTML document or via a code module for *Page Builders*. This reduces the time needed to display the main content.

**Delayed or asynchronous JavaScript**: JavaScript scripts can delay rendering. Use the *async* or *defer* attribute to load non-essential scripts after the initial rendering. However, be careful, as this can affect the behavior of certain functions.

**Resource prioritization**: Determine which resources (images, scripts, styles) are needed immediately and ensure that they are loaded first. This can be done by adjusting the order of the <link> and <script> tags in the HTML code.

**Font optimization**: If your page uses custom fonts, make sure you load only the variants needed for initial rendering. Avoid loading unused fonts that could make loading more cumbersome.

8. **Fast server**
Choose a high-performance web host and make sure that the server responds quickly.

9. **Reducing redirects**
Avoid unnecessary redirects, which can slow down page loading.

10. **Using Gzip/Brotli compression**
Activate compression to reduce the size of transferred files.

# CHOOSING A WORDPRESS THEME

When you create a WordPress site, the choice of theme is crucial. Here are some important points to bear in mind when choosing the right theme:

1. **Regular updates.**
   Opt for a theme that is regularly updated to ensure compatibility with new versions of WordPress and recent coding standards. This guarantees the long-term security and stability of your site.

2. **Reliable technical support.**
   Choose a theme developed by a reputable team or developers who offer responsive technical support when needed. Active support forums and well-maintained knowledge bases are positive signs.

3. **Performance and loading speed.**
   prioritize themes that focus on performance and loading speed. Good optimization contributes to a better user experience and helps your site's SEO.

4. **Easy customization.**
   Look for a theme that is versatile and easy to customize. It should offer a variety of layout options, colors and fonts, and allow design tweaks without requiring advanced coding skills.

5. **Solid development practices.**
   Check that the theme follows good development practices, such as using semantic HTML tags and optimizing the code for performance.

6. **Plugin compatibility.**
   Make sure the theme is compatible with the essential plugins you plan to use to extend your site's functionality.

7. **Demo test.**
   Before committing yourself, test the theme demo to evaluate its appearance, user-friendliness, and functionality. Make sure that it meets your needs in terms of design and functionality, and that it will be able to evolve with your future needs, even if they arise several months or years from now. Also bear in mind the potential recurring costs of major theme updates.

# PAGE BUILDERS

Also consider the various *Page Builders*. A Page Builder theme is designed to work seamlessly with independent modules for building and laying out even complex, customized pages without having to write any code. This is one of their great strengths. *Page Builders* often offer a wide variety of customization options for page layout, colors, fonts and other visual aspects, allowing users to create unique and attractive designs that are close to the look and feel of paper magazines. They include pre-designed page templates and ready-to-use sections to make it easy to create professional websites quickly. What's more, responsive and adaptive modes for all media, such as smartphones and tablets, are native. This saves a considerable amount of development time.

In terms of performance optimization, although *Page Builders* can add a certain amount of overhead to page loading, they are often optimized - or offer the possibility of being optimized - to maintain good performance in terms of loading speed and search engine optimization.

In short, choosing a Page Builder offers a combination of design flexibility, advanced features, and ease of use, making it a popular choice for users who want to create custom websites without having to master coding.

*Divi*[44] and ***Elementor***[45] are two of the most popular *Page Builders* for WordPress, offering similar functionality but with slightly different approaches, particularly in terms of user interface, features, and performance. The choice between the two will often depend on the user's personal preferences and the specific needs of the project. It's worth noting that both have extensive libraries of plugins to further enhance their native capabilities.

The main disadvantage of *Page Builders* is that they are not open source, and you will have to pay a license fee to use them. What's more, the content injected into Wordpress cannot be exported and used on another Wordpress site that does not use the same *Page Builder*. The page layout in block and section mode is part of the content. But this is a rather rare case of use (complete site redesign on a new platform in the future, for example).

Whichever theme you choose, you need to create a child theme[46] associated with the main theme. The child theme will allow you to modify the *functions.php* parameter file to add certain commands and filters to make Wordpress as lightweight as possible.

---

[44] https://www.elegantthemes.com

[45] https://elementor.com

[46] https://www.hostinger.com/tutorials/how-to-create-wordpress-child-theme

Chapter V

# SUSTAINABLE
# OF CONTENT

Managing the content of a website can have a significant impact on its environmental footprint, both when it is first inserted and when it is managed for the long term.

The eco-responsibility of a website is not only measured at the design stage, but also, and above all, during its lifetime. Each time new content is added, a number of aspects need to be taken into account to ensure that the site does not gradually slow down, and its initial optimization is reduced to nothing.

# DATA DURABILITY

Content management is not just about publishing and organizing information. It also encompasses data sustainability. Remember to check your content to unpublish and delete anything that is obsolete. This also applies to downloaded media. It is pointless and energetically costly to keep images that no longer appear on the site, especially when you realize that software such as Wordpress can create up to ten versions of the same image, with different sizes, to display them according to the context.

When you need to delete obsolete content, you should regularly clean up your database. Plugins such as *Autoptimize*[47] for Wordpress allow you to carry out these clean-ups easily and free of charge.

---

[47] https://fr.wordpress.org/plugins/autoptimize/

# SEARCH ENGINE OPTIMISATION (SEO) AND CONTENT ORGANISATION

So what happens when you delete obsolete content? In the past, search engine optimization revolved almost entirely around keywords. A few decades ago, SEO agencies would identify keywords and write an article containing them as often as possible, creating *back* links from other websites containing the same keywords in the anchor text.

Although this is still partly true today, Google, to name but one, has come a long way as a search engine. It no longer simply displays results when the keywords syntactically match the user's query. On the contrary, thanks to artificial intelligence, it now understands at a semantic level what the user is looking for and displays results that correspond to the search intention.

Obsolete content should no longer be referenced, as its weighting in search volumes is decreasing.

**Good SEO is sustainable.**

It helps businesses to develop in the long term and profitably. It is socially sustainable because it helps Internet users find what they are looking for. And it's environmentally sustainable because it reduces the need for users to visit several other, potentially less environmentally friendly, websites.

By organizing your content into clusters, i.e. introductory articles that link to related, in-depth articles, and vice versa, you can respond to users' secondary search intent. While primary search intent is about meeting the user's immediate need, secondary search intent is about answering other questions that the user encounters during their research. Content groupings and internal links can help to meet secondary search intent, saving the user from having to return to Google and carry out another web search.

However, a website with perfect SEO will attract a lot of traffic, which will emit a lot of carbon. However, users will search anyway, with or without your sustainable website. If your 'perfect' website is greener than the rest and is the only website that users need to visit, this will save even more carbon emissions on a macro scale. To do this, keep an eye on the bounce rate of your content pages. The higher it is, the more likely it is that your visitors won't find what they're looking for but have landed on one of your pages all the same.

## ON THE DESIGN SIDE, OPT FOR MINIMALISM

Minimalist design is an approach that has been gaining in popularity in the field of web design for several years. Its fundamental principle is that "less is more". In practical terms, this means creating sites that are clean, simple and functional, where each element has a clear role, and the user experience comes first. By eliminating superfluous visual elements, this approach allows users to concentrate fully on the information or message being presented.

In minimalist design, the strategic use of negative space is essential. Leaving empty areas creates visual balance and improves legibility. This emptiness highlights the main content and avoids visual confusion, making reading more pleasant and easier to understand.

Simple, legible typography is also important. By using clear, unadorned fonts, you ensure that the text reads smoothly and pleasantly, highlighting the text and improving the transmission of information.

In terms of colors, minimalist design is limited to a small number of colors to maintain a clean, consistent aesthetic. This avoids visual confusion and highlights the key elements of the content.

Finally, minimalist design uses a visual hierarchy to guide the user's attention. By playing with the size, color and layout of elements, it highlights important information, creates a clear visual structure and makes content easier to understand. In short, minimalist design makes navigation more intuitive and improves the user experience by visually organizing information in a clear and effective way.

# 3-CLICK RULE

A basic rule of website ergonomics is to make information accessible in no more than 3 clicks. The underlying idea seems perfectly relevant: too many clicks to reach information is destabilizing for the user. If they feel lost or discouraged, they are likely to go to another site to find the information they are initially looking for.

Introduced at a time when it took several seconds to go from one page to another, limiting the number of steps provided an "illusory" guarantee of limiting the time it took to find information. This law has gradually been abandoned, and there are now many sites with multi-level tree navigation.

However, at a time when the use of bandwidth is becoming a major ecological asset, this issue is making a comeback. Reaching information in 3 clicks means that Internet users only must change pages 3 times, and the difference in terms of energy costs is not negligible.

Of course, it can be difficult to formulate a maximum of 3 levels of navigation when you're managing a site with a lot of content. This is where the internal links linking content together come into their own. From the content of an article or the display of related content, you can navigate across the site to other tree structures without having to return to the home page.

Another way of managing total access to content is to take care of the internal search engine and list the results by relevance. Wordpress natively allows the integration of an internal search engine, and this is excellent news. There are, of course, ways of going even further in this area, but the native search field in which you type a series of keywords is, in most cases, sufficient.

# MINIMISE THE CUMULATIVE OFFSET OF THE LAYOUT (*CUMULATIVE LAYOUT SHIFT*)

Cumulative layout shift (CLS) occurs when layout elements move during the loading process of a web page.

This generally occurs when elements with long loading times are placed on top of elements with faster loading times, such as images, embedded elements, advertisements, and dynamically injected content, such as contact forms or content discovery modules ("you may also be interested in this").

Sustainable websites take care to define the dimensions of each relevant element using the *height* and *width* attributes in the style sheet. This makes the page experience smoother, improves visibility in Google (a metric present in the *Core Web Vitals*) and reduces some of the greenhouse gas emissions associated with excessively long loading times or frustrated users.

# IMAGE OPTIMISATION

Before trying to optimize your images, check whether you could do away with some of them instead. For example, there may be decorative images that a sustainable website doesn't really need, or redundant images that don't add any value because they're too like other images on the same web page.

There are several ways to reduce the size of images. One simple method, which doesn't require much technical installation, is to upload your images to *tinypng.com*[48] . This is a free online **PNG** and **JPEG** compression service, as well as **WebP**, the new compression format developed by Google teams.

The **SVG** format also offers native compression since it is a vector format with no loss of quality when the visual is reduced or enlarged. Ideal for logos, maps, or icons. Beware, however, of the security associated with SVG files. You'll need a dedicated plugin such as *Safe SVG*[49] .

If your website runs on WordPress and you prefer to optimize your images in an eco-friendly way directly in the CMS, you can opt for dedicated plugins such as *Imagify*[50] , *ShortPixel*[51] , *TinyPNG*[38] or *EWWW*[52] . These plugins also include an easy way of implementing '*lazy loading*', which consists of

---

[48] https://tinypng.com
[49] https://wordpress.org/plugins/safe-svg/
[50] https://imagify.io/fr/
[51] https://shortpixel.com
[52] https://ewww.io

postponing the display of off-screen images and thus improving the speed of your web pages.

From a socially sustainable point of view, we recommend entering alternative texts. Alternative texts (alt tags) are descriptions of images that appear when the user cannot see them. For example, a visually impaired user may have a screen reader that reads the alt text, or the browser will display the alt text if the internet connection is not sufficient to load the image.

# VIDEO AND PODCAST OPTIMISATION

Videos, podcasts, and all media files other than traditional images are extremely demanding in terms of storage resources and, above all, bandwidth. It is absolutely not recommended to host them yourself on your own site. Especially as optimizing the size of the files or the streaming stream can really cause problems with loss of quality.

To do this, leave it to dedicate platforms such as *YouTube* or *Vimeo* for video, *Podcaststics* for podcasts with the appropriate relays on audio streaming platforms such as Spotify, Deezer etc. These platforms take care of compressing the files, creating the preview thumbnail and, above all, distributing the rendering to the target communities - if you so choose. Private mode is also perfectly suitable.

All that remains is to integrate the video or podcast player into the website, and the platforms mentioned above show how to do this without difficulty. Beware, however, that integrating this type of player can sometimes require a lot of JavaScript resources to be loaded with the player, as well as a battery of marketing cookies. The alternative would be to offer a simple image representative of your media (cover image of the video or podcast), add a "play" button in the center and link to the external native page of your media. This saves you a considerable amount of energy. What's more, if you opt to create a YouTube channel or a Spotify creator account, you can offer your visitors all your multimedia elements.

# SIMPLIFY FONTS

Web fonts are popular because they can have a positive impact on user loyalty and brand image. Legibility and intelligibility are key attributes of a good web font.

However, web fonts must be downloaded like any other file to be displayed correctly. The environmental impact of a non-system font in terms of greenhouse gas emissions is comparable to that of a small image.

That's why we recommend you stick to a maximum of two web fonts. One for the title and one for the body of your content. You can optimize most fonts by compressing them. These web font files are stored locally on the website's disk space. In this way, visitors do not have to download them from a third-party server, such as *Google Fonts*, and it is possible to control their compression (NB: This does not apply to *Adobe* fonts, which are not eligible for download and direct use).

If you want to go even further and reduce the environmental impact of font downloads on your website to zero, you can stick to web-safe system fonts such as Arial, Verdana or Times New Roman[53] .

---

[53] https://kinsta.com/fr/blog/polices-caracteres-web-safe/

# DELETE EMOTICONS

In WordPress, if you don't intend to use emoticons, you can deactivate them and their scripts in the *functions.php* file of your child theme. This will save you a considerable amount of time in pre-loading your pages:

```
/* Disable the emoji's */
function disable_emojis() {
remove_action( 'wp_head', 'print_emoji_detec-
tion_script', 7 );
remove_action( 'admin_print_scripts', 'print_emoji_de-
tection_script' );
remove_action( 'wp_print_styles', 'print_emoji_styles'
);
remove_action( 'admin_print_styles',
'print_emoji_styles' );
remove_filter( 'the_content_feed', 'wp_staticize_emo-
ji' );
remove_filter( 'comment_text_rss', 'wp_staticize_emo-
ji' );
remove_filter( 'wp_mail', 'wp_stati-
cize_emoji_for_email' );
add_filter( 'tiny_mce_plugins', 'disable_emojis_ti-
nymce' );
add_filter( 'wp_resource_hints', 'disable_emojis_re-
move_dns_prefetch', 10, 2 );
}
add_action( 'init', 'disable_emojis' );

/* Filter function used to remove the tinymce emoji
plugin.
*
* @param array $plugins
* @return array Difference betwen the two arrays
*/
function disable_emojis_tinymce( $plugins ) {
if ( is_array( $plugins ) ) {
return array_diff( $plugins, array( 'wpemoji' ) );
} else {
return array();
}
}
/* Remove emoji CDN hostname from DNS prefetching
hints.
*
```

```
* @param array $urls URLs to print for resource hints.
* @param string $relation_type The relation type the
URLs are printed for.
* @return array Difference betwen the two arrays.
*/
function disable_emojis_remove_dns_prefetch( $urls,
$relation_type ) {
if ( 'dns-prefetch' == $relation_type ) {
/* This filter is documented in wp-includes/format-
ting.php */
$emoji_svg_url = apply_filters( 'emoji_svg_url',
'https://s.w.org/images/core/emoji/2/svg/' );

$urls = array_diff( $urls, array( $emoji_svg_url ) );
 }
return $urls;
}
```

As is often the case with Wordpress, there is the *Disable Emo-jis* plugin[54] which allows you to do this without a single line of code.

---

[54] https://wordpress.org/plugins/disable-emojis/

# REL='PRECONNECT' ATTRIBUTE

The *preconnect* attribute can be used to speed up the loading of important resources in the calculation of the *Large Contentfull Paint* element in *Web Core Vitals*.

For example, when a CSS style sheet requires a font to be loaded, once the CSS file has been loaded, DNS, TCP and TLS exchanges should normally be carried out first with the source of the font, and only then can the font itself be loaded.

With *preconnect*, DNS, TCP and TLS exchanges for the font can be carried out in parallel with the process of loading the CSS file, so that once the process of loading the CSS file is complete, only the font file itself needs to be loaded.

# DEBUG MODE AND LOG COLLECTION

All kinds of logging methods add to loading time and server resources, since it is necessary to record data in real time about visits. We're not talking here about your visitors' statistical data, which is generally stored on a third-party service (*Google Analytics* etc.). In this case, the data is collected off-site and has no influence on the caching of elements delivered to visitors.

Although this can be useful during the development of the site to understand 5xx errors in particular, it is necessary to completely remove logs (database audit, Wordpress audit, log of emails sent etc.) and debug modes once the site has gone into production.

# THE DARK MODE

The principle behind *Dark Mode* is to offer a dark version of a site's pages in terms of design, either automatically, depending on the browser settings, or manually, *via* a dedicated button.

The initial objective is to increase reading comfort in poorly lit areas. However, several studies have shown that dark mode impairs reading comprehension.

From an ecological point of view, dark colors are likely to consume less energy. For technical reasons, websites in dark mode consume the same amount of energy as sites in light mode on backlit LED screens. Only OLED screens can save energy on dark websites, but they are not very widespread.

If OLED screens remain a top-of-the-range product and are widely unavailable, you shouldn't set up a dark mode to save energy. Think about the financial costs and greenhouse gas emissions associated with redesigning the dark mode: the colors, styles and images on your website will have to be adapted or even duplicated.

# THE PAGE WEIGHT BUDGET METHOD

A page weight budget is literally a budget for the weight of a web page. Not in grams of course, but in kilobytes or mega-bytes of files. More precisely, it is the size of the files trans-ferred over the Internet when a web page is loaded.

Once the budget has been set, the aim is to deliver each key page of the website within the agreed budget, ideally by re-ducing it. This is a clear point of reference to focus on when planning, designing, and developing the site.

There are online tools for pre-calculating the *Page Weight Budget*, such as the *Performance Budget Calculator*[55] . It pro-vides concrete figures based on your needs.

By simply introducing the concept of the page weight budget at the website design stage, and then each time the site is redesigned or adapted, it becomes a way of thinking and working that goes so far as to guide decisions. For example, there are already 3 large images on this page, is there still room for a 4th?

---

[55] https://www.performancebudget.io

# IMPACT OF ONLINE ADVERTISING AND SUSTAINABLE ALTERNATIVES

Online advertising is often resource-intensive and can make a significant contribution to a website's environmental footprint for several reasons:

### Loading Rich Content

Online advertisements are often designed to be attractive and interactive, which means that they may contain elements such as high-resolution images, high-definition videos, complex animations, and sophisticated scripts. Loading this rich content requires a significant amount of bandwidth and processing power, which can lead to high energy consumption by servers and user devices.

### Monitoring and targeting

Online advertising frequently uses tracking and targeting technologies to collect data about users, such as their browsing behavior, interests and purchasing habits. These technologies often involve the use of cookies, scripts and other mechanisms that increase the processing load on the server and client side, which can lead to increased energy consumption.

### Advertising networks

Online advertising is often distributed via ad networks, which aggregate and deliver ads on a large scale across numerous websites. These ad networks use complex infrastructures of servers and data centers to deliver the ads efficiently, resulting in significant energy consumption.

### Dynamic updating
Many online advertisements are designed to update dynamically depending on the user's actions or changes in the content of the web page. This can require continuous communication between the user's browser and the ad servers, resulting in increased energy consumption.

### Redirections and tracking
Online advertisements can sometimes result in multiple redirections to other websites or landing pages, which increases the processing load and bandwidth consumption. In addition, the tracking mechanisms used in ads can generate additional network traffic, contributing to higher energy consumption.

In short, online advertising can have a significant impact on a website's environmental footprint due to its intensive use of resources, particularly in terms of bandwidth, processing power and energy. It is therefore essential for website publishers and advertisers to take these aspects into account when designing and delivering online advertising, and to look for solutions that minimize their impact on the environment.

There are several alternatives to traditional online advertising that can be less resource-intensive and reduce a website's environmental footprint.

### Text ads

Text ads are simple ads consisting mainly of text, with no additional multimedia content such as images or videos. They generally require less bandwidth and processing power, making them a lighter alternative in terms of energy consumption.

### Static ads

Static ads are ads that do not change or rarely change, which means that they do not need to be dynamically updated and therefore generate less network traffic. These ads can be less resource-intensive than dynamic or interactive ads.

### Local or contextual advertising

Rather than serving generic ads to a large audience, website publishers can opt for more targeted and relevant ads based on the user's geographical location or the content of the web page on which the ads are displayed. This can reduce the need to collect and process large amounts of user data, contributing to a smaller environmental footprint.

### Self-hosted ads

Instead of using third-party advertising networks, website publishers can choose to host their own ads themselves. This gives them total control over ad content and can reduce dependency on external advertising infrastructures, which are potentially less environmentally friendly.

**Alternative monetization models**

Instead of relying solely on advertising to generate revenue, it is worth exploring other monetization models, such as subscriptions, donations, digital products or paid services. These models can reduce dependency on online advertising and contribute to a lighter, less intrusive user experience.

By adopting these alternatives, website publishers can reduce the environmental impact of their online activity while offering a quality user experience. It is also important for advertisers to support these initiatives by adjusting their advertising strategies to minimize their ecological footprint. Ultimately, the transition to more sustainable advertising practices is beneficial both for the environment and for the sustainability of the digital industry.

Chapter VI

# ACCESSIBILITY

Website accessibility aims to make websites usable by everyone, regardless of disability. This encompasses aspects such as keyboard navigation, screen reader support and inclusive design. Indeed, all individuals should have equal access and opportunities on the web, as this is considered a fundamental human right. In this way, not only people with disabilities are supported, but also the elderly, people living in rural areas and people in developing countries.

Most common categories of disability:

- **Motor skills/physical impairments.** Users may find it difficult to move certain parts of their body, to make precise movements (for example when using a mouse).

- **Photosensitive seizures.** Conditions such as epilepsy can cause seizures, which are often triggered by flashing lights.

- **Cognitive disorders.** There are also many conditions that affect cognitive abilities, such as dementia and dyslexia.

- **Visual impairment.** This includes a partial or total inability to see or perceive color contrasts.

- **Hearing impairment.** Some users have reduced hearing capacity.

# GRAPHICS AND PUBLICATIONS

## Text

When communicating online or in print, text is your main tool for ensuring that your audience receives information effectively. However, different texts serve different purposes and it's important to bear in mind that some formats aren't always effective for communicating our information.

- Fonts should be easy to read, visible and simple. When using a font, bear in mind that the simpler it is, the easier it will be for someone to read it. Serif, cursive and italic fonts are more difficult to read, especially for people with cognitive difficulties such as dyslexia. We recommend using Sans Serif fonts such as Arial, Calibri, Century Gothic, Helvetica, Tahoma, and Verdana.

- Font sizes must be responsive, which means that the user must be able to choose a font size that is more comfortable to read.

- Use left-aligned text instead of justified text, as justified text makes reading more difficult for dyslexics.

- If you want to emphasize your text, use bold letters. Italics and underlining are difficult to read for some people with cognitive disabilities.

- Include spaces between paragraphs to help people follow the rhythm and general idea of the text.

**Images**

Images can be used to convey a specific meaning or feeling. At other times, they can be used to simplify complex ideas. In any case, someone using a screen reader needs to know what the image means. For this reason, all images must be accompanied by an alternative text or "alt".

Alternative text is a written description that accompanies an image. Visually impaired people use alternative text to "see" the content of an image using text-to-speech tools.

This alt text is also widely used for referencing images in search engines. A simple image whose only role is to add color or breathing space to the content, without being semantically linked to it, should be avoided. This will improve referencing, simplicity, and bandwidth. Don't use it on decorative images. To put it simply, don't use this tool for elements of your website that don't really offer any information. It's confusing for screen readers and keyboard users.

Be precise and equivalent by presenting the same content and function as those shown in the image.

Do not use the expressions "image of..." or "graphic of..." to describe the image. It is generally obvious to the user that it is an image.

Do not use it for images accompanied by a link. If the image and the link led to the same website, the screen reader will read the same text twice, which is not practical for the user. Our aim is to remove obstacles, not add new ones. Keep it short. Some screen readers find it difficult to read more than 125 characters, so try to keep the alternative text short but complete.

If the image is really complex, two alternative texts must be provided, a simple definition and a long description explaining the structured information.

Use captioning for images. Text next to an image can help provide more context. Image captioning is recognized by screen readers. Do not use alternative text if there is an image caption. Using both alternative text and image captions makes the content repetitive for people using a screen reader. Describe what you are captioning. This is important for people who don't have access to the image itself. They need to be able to understand what image you are captioning. Make sure your caption is clear and detailed.

Avoid text in an image if you want the text to be identifiable by screen readers. Text as an image is not ideal for people who use magnifiers, as enlarging the text in an image could lead to a pixelated result.

If you need to use text as an image, consider using alternative text or image subtitles and SVG (Scalable Vector Graphics).

**Graphics**

To avoid any complications, graphics should always include an element other than color to help understand its content (such as icons of various shapes or text descriptions), to allow color-blind people the same reading comfort.

Maintain a high contrast between background and foreground colors. A minimum contrast ratio of 4.5:1 in relation to the background color is recommended by the World Wide Web Consortium (W3C).

# WEB SITES

## Controls

Controls, also known as user interface elements (UI elements), include any element with which the user can interact on your website. The most common controls are buttons and links.

- Controls that are too small or too close together can be annoying for users of small touch screens, such as smartphones.

- The controls must include an indicative text to indicate their use.

## Page layout

- The structural layout of your website is of major importance for people who use their keyboard to navigate it. Make sure your website has a simple and complete layout.

- Avoid sudden changes to the presentation of your website. Inform your audience before implementing any structural or visual changes.

- Images must always be accompanied by a description and alternative text, and videos must always have a transcript.

- Follow a logical and linear arrangement of content elements.

- Always write descriptive links and titles and avoid expressions like "Click here".

**Compatible with keyboard**

The most common way of navigating using a keyboard is to use the Tab key. This will allow you to move from one area of a page to another that may have "keyboard focus", which includes links, buttons, and forms. Your aim should therefore be to ensure that all web content and navigation is accessible using the Tab key.

**Colors**

You need to make sure that the colors you select for your site contrast well so that everyone can distinguish the different elements of the page. The most pressing issue is to ensure that the text stands out against the background. Ideally, you should contrast a dark color with a light color, making sure that they don't mix.

## Headers

Clear headings help screen readers to interpret your pages. This makes it much easier to navigate around the page. It's also easy to do because all you must do is make sure you use the correct title levels in your content.

## Forms

The most important thing is to ensure that each field is clearly labelled. You should also aim to place the labels next to the respective fields. Although a sighted user can easily associate a label with the corresponding field or option, this may not be obvious to someone using a screen reader.

## Automatic navigation

Understanding how to pause an auto-playing video can be difficult when using a screen reader, and some users may be confused or even frightened by the sudden noise. You should therefore avoid including elements that start without the user asking.

**Text-to-speech**

Think about adding a text-to-speech facility to your website so that people can listen to its content. With a clearly hierarchical HTML rendering, the work is often already done in this respect.

**Text resizing**

Make it possible for people who might need it.

**Understandable links**

Use descriptive language on your hyperlinks.

**Easy to read page**

An "*easy to read*" page is a web page designed to be easily understood by a wide range of people, including those with reading or comprehension difficulties or cognitive disabilities. Here are some features and strategies for creating such a page:

1. **Simple, clear language**
   Use simple, direct language. Avoid technical terms and jargon. Use short sentences and familiar words.

2. **Clear structure**

   Organize the content logically using descriptive headings and sub-headings. Use bulleted lists for important information.

3. **Legible font size and style**

   Use a simple, easy-to-read font. Make sure the font size is large enough to be readable, generally around 16px or more.

4. **High contrast**

   Make sure there is good contrast between the text and the background to make it easier to read, especially for people with impaired vision. Use contrasting colors for text and background.

5. **Significant images and media**

   Use images and media that reinforce the content and make it easier to understand. Make sure you include alternative descriptions (alt attribute) for images, so that they are accessible to screen readers.

6. **Avoid distractions**

   Limit the use of visual or interactive elements that could distract the user from understanding the main content.

### 7. Make navigation easier

Make sure that navigation on the page is intuitive and simple. Use descriptive links to guide users to other relevant sections of the site.

### 8. Test accessibility

Use accessibility evaluation tools to test your page and identify potential problems. Carry out tests with users with specific needs to obtain concrete feedback.

By implementing these strategies, you can create accessible web pages that are easy to read and understand for all users, whatever their skill level or abilities.

It can also be a single page in easy-to-read mode describing your content, your services and how to contact you.

# RESPONSIVE DESIGN

With over 50% of online users using a smartphone, "responsive" mode has become compulsory in recent years.

The principle is to redistribute the content elements on a page according to the device on which the page is being read. There are 3 distinct screen formats: the smartphone with a screen width of less than 728 pixels, the tablet with a screen width of between 728 and 1023 pixels and the desktop with a screen width of at least 1024 pixels.

Most *Page Builders* tools offer this mode natively. However, you will need to manually check that each page is displayed correctly on all 3 screen widths to avoid any surprises.

Chapter VII

# OUTLOOK

Accurately predicting future trends in sustainable development on the web is a difficult exercise, but here are a few possible directions in which the industry could evolve:

## Blockchain for sustainability

Blockchain technology offers greater traceability and transparency, which could be used to verify sustainable practices throughout the digital supply chain, including hosting, site development and online advertising.

### Artificial intelligence for ecological optimization

Artificial intelligence can be used to proactively analyze data and identify opportunities for ecological optimization, such as reducing server energy consumption, improving the effectiveness of online advertising and personalizing recommendations to encourage sustainable behavior.

### Renewable energy in web infrastructure

Web hosting companies could step up their efforts to migrate to renewable energy sources to power their data centers, thereby reducing the carbon footprint of web infrastructure.

### Analysis of the environmental impact of websites

Tools for analyzing the environmental impact of websites could become more commonplace, enabling developers and site owners to quantify and minimize the carbon footprint of their digital platforms.

**Extended liability**

Consumers and users could put increasing pressure on companies to adopt sustainable practices, which would encourage web companies to integrate environmental considerations into all their activities.

**Digital circular economy**

The adoption of circular economy practices, such as re-using, sharing, and recycling digital assets, could become more widespread in the web industry, helping to reduce digital waste.

**Standards and regulations**

Governments and regulators could introduce stricter digital sustainability standards and regulations, forcing companies to report on their environmental impact and adopt more environmentally friendly practices.

These emerging trends represent potential areas where the web industry could evolve in an increasingly sustainable and environmentally responsible manner. However, achieving these goals will ultimately depend on businesses, governments, civil society organizations and consumers working together to transform the web industry into a positive force for a more sustainable future.

# SUSTAINABLE DEVELOPMENT COMMUNITIES ON THE INTERNET

There are several communities committed to sustainable web development, bringing together like-minded professionals, developers, designers, and enthusiasts. Here are just a few of them:

### Green Web Foundation[56]

The Green Web Foundation is an international organization that aims to make the web more sustainable by encouraging the use of renewable energy to power websites. They provide resources, tools, and information to help businesses and developers adopt more environmentally friendly practices.

### Sustainable Web Manifesto[57]

The Sustainable Web Manifesto is a community project that aims to promote sustainable web development by encouraging the adoption of best practices such as lightweight design, performance optimization and the

---

[56] https://www.thegreenwebfoundation.org
[57] https://www.sustainablewebmanifesto.com

use of renewable energy. Developers can sign up to the manifesto and commit to following its principles.

## Sustainable Web Design Community[58]

This community brings together web design and development professionals to share resources, case studies and advice on green web design. They also organize events and workshops to raise awareness and educate people about sustainable web development.

## ClimateAction.Tech[59]

ClimateAction.Tech is a global community of technology professionals working together to mitigate climate change through concrete action. They provide a space to share resources, projects, and ideas on how technology can be used to support environmental sustainability, including in the field of web development.

---

[58] https://www.w3.org/community/sustyweb/
[59] https://climateaction.tech

# CONCLUSION

The central notion to emerge from this exploration is that sustainability on the web is not simply an option, but a compelling necessity. The environmental impacts of the digital sector, combined with social and ethical issues, require a fundamental re-evaluation of the way we design, develop, and manage our websites.

Eco-design, performance optimization, responsible hosting, accessibility, and many other aspects have been examined to reveal their transformative potential. However, the transition to a sustainable web is not without its challenges. Emerging trends, the implications of future technologies, and social issues require constant vigilance and active collaboration. The solutions proposed in this book offer perspectives, but their implementation depends largely on the commitment of the web development community.

This book ends with a call to action. It invites developers, businesses, educators, and decision-makers to join a dynamic community dedicated to sustainable development on the Internet. Together, we can share our knowledge, solve emerging challenges, and shape a future where the web becomes an engine for sustainable progress.

In conclusion, sustainable development on the web is not just a technical quest, but a moral and strategic imperative. It is an invitation to rethink the way we design our digital spaces, bearing in mind that every line of code, every compressed image, and every choice of hosting contribute to forging a digital future that is more respectful of our planet and its inhabitants.

Every action counts.

# APPENDIX
# CHECKLIST BEFORE PUTTING
# YOUR SITE ONLINE.

In addition to all the points we have considered to-gether in this book, here is a list of checks you must make before putting your site online to avoid any surprises, particularly in terms of natural referencing and security.

## GLOBAL

- Consistency of section titles in the main menu.

- Presence of favicon and icons for smartphones.

- Mention of social networks.

- SEO check on each page.

- The image on the front page of each page is present and corresponds in format and quality to the standards for sharing images.

- Checking the script and tags for analytics.

- The SSL certificate is in place and links to the site are forced *via* HTTPS.

- The notification banner on the use of cookies is in place and non-consent does indeed delete cookies.

- Are the images optimized and dynamically compressed?

- The site is responsive on tablets and smartphones on all pages.

- Testing of contact forms with actual receipt of submissions by e-mail and/or actual registration in the database.

- Forms must state what is done with the data entered and sent.

- Anti-spam protection.

- Copyright at foot of page.

- *The Cookie policy* and *Privacy policy* pages are accessible and correctly described.

- The writing styles and positioning of elements are uniform on all pages.

- In the case of a site redesign, the 301 redirect links for the old content are still in place.

- The menu logo links to the home page.

- *Robots.txt* and *sitemap.xml* files for referencing.

- Page Speed Insight gives an average result of over 80%.

- Presence of page 404.

- The site is free of broken links *via* brokenlink-check.com.

- The back office is secure and behind a firewall.

- The site is available with and without "www".

- Page content is cached.

- Recurring files can be accessed *via* a CDN.

- The site description is correctly integrated.

- *Google search console* and *Bing Master Tool* are configured.

- Page URLs are meaningful and semantic.

- Error messages on forms are translated into the language of the site.

- Meta data for sharing on social networks is defined (*featured image + excerpt*) for all types of content.

## WORDPRESS

- The main theme and the children's theme have their own visual and the author's reference is given.

- Unused plugins and themes are deleted.

- The Wordpress code, themes and plugins are all automatically updated.

- The administrator role with its valid and accessible e-mail address is properly documented with a strong password.

- The native Wordpress *health site* gives a decent result.

# ACCOMMODATION

- FTP, sFTP and SSH accesses are documented.

- You can access the hosting cluster to change the PHP version, for example to the latest version.

- The prefix of the database tables is not the standard "wp_" and has been modified.

- DNS access is documented.

# TABLE OF CONTENTS

## PERFORMANCE OPTIMISATION    41

## SUSTAINABLE OF CONTENT    57